THIS BOOK RECORDS THE FIRST YEARS OF

Baby Record Book

Illustrations by Lucy Su

✦ ✦ ✦

Text by Karen Farrington

ABBEYDALE PRESS

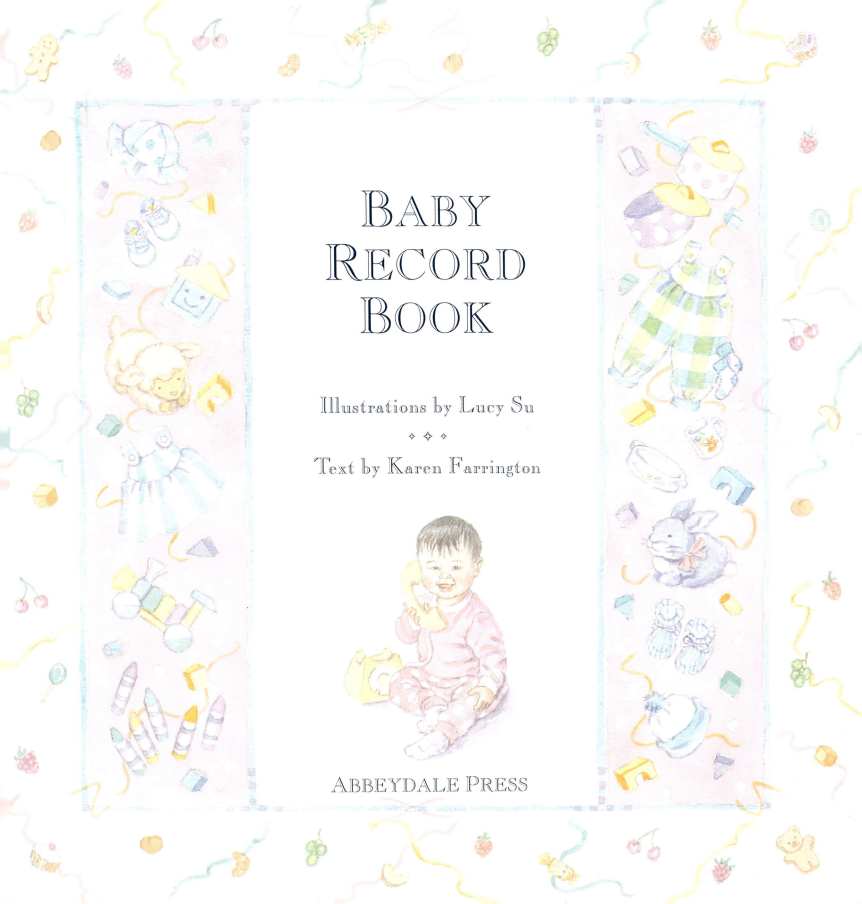

CONTENTS

✦ ✦ ✦

Family Tree 8

First Hours 10

Welcome to Our World 12

Coming Home 14

Telling the World 16

Baby Firsts 18

Lullaby 20

Rub-a-dub-dub 22

Naming Day 24

Special People 26

Play Time 28

Favourite Toys 30

Let's Go 32

First Foods 34

Happy Talk 36

First Friends 38

Favourite Things 40

Summer Fun 42

Setting Off 44

Art Work 46

Party Pieces 48

Celebrations 50

The First Noel 52

Happy Birthday to You 54

Predictions 56

Medical Records 58

Growing Up 60

FAMILY TREE

With every new addition comes a fresh branch on the family tree.
Record previous generations here, they will fascinate
your child in years to come.

Grandfather (maternal)   Grandfather (paternal)

_____   _____

Grandmother (maternal)   Grandmother (paternal)

Uncles and Aunts

_____   _____

_____   _____

Cousins

_____   _____

_____   _____

_____   _____

First Hours

After months of waiting, baby has arrived. All the anticipation and anxiety about your unborn baby vanish as you hold your little bundle close for the first time. For parents there is soaring joy, excitement – and relief too! Note down details of that unforgettable moment here.

Date and day of birth	Did baby cry?
Time	Baby's special features
Place	Baby's first clothes
Due date	Father's first thought
Delivered by	Mother's first thought
Weight	Other comments
Length	
Head measurement	Birth registered (place and date)
Hair?	

WELCOME TO OUR WORLD

✧ ✧ ✧

A new baby spreads happiness and hope among everyone. It's not only mum and dad who cherish the first hours and days of the new arrival. After the drama of the delivery is over, close family and friends are longing for their first glimpse of baby's bright eyes and tiny toes. With them comes a shower of good wishes and gifts, each rattle, matinee jacket and pair of bootees carefully chosen to say in a special way: 'We're pleased to meet you'. Mum often finds herself festooned with beautiful blooms and, who knows, maybe some champagne by way of congratulations. Amid all the excitement it is easy to forget who featured in those first few days. On the next page, write down your list of visitors and the names of those who sent gifts and flowers.

Visitors and presents

COMING HOME

Today is the start of your time together as a family.
Soon you will not recall what life was like
without having a baby to love.

Bonds which will last a lifetime are being forged in these initial weeks.
Ahead lies laughter, sharing, caring — and a few tears. Take each day and
night as it comes and enjoy this first adventure in the world together.

Date and time

Was baby awake or asleep?

Weather

Describe the nursery

How did you get home?

What was baby wearing?

Was anyone there to greet you both?

When did baby feed?

Photographs

Telling The World

✦ ✦ ✦

It's time to broadcast the good news. Anyone who knows you have been pregnant will be eager to hear the details. Some people advertise in local or national newspapers while others send cards to distant relatives and far flung friends. Just picture their faces breaking into huge smiles after they pick up the card from the doormat and read all about baby. Don't forget to include all of baby's vital statistics: full name, weight and date and time of birth. Attach your chosen card and published newspaper advertisement on the next page.

Arrival card
◆ ◇ ◆
Newspaper cutting

BABY FIRSTS

Every day brings a new discovery for infants. They grow ever
more aware of what is going on around them – and
strive to be a part of it.

Before them lies a huge array of 'firsts' to thrill them. And for parents
it is a magical time too. Babies are an endless fascination. Who would have
thought a baby sucking its thumb for the first time could be such a wonderful
sight? Yet your heart thuds with pride at every early achievement, equally
vital as those of later years. Record those moments here before
they are lost in the mists of time.

First smile

_____

Who was it for?

_____

First focuses on a moving object

_____

First finds hands

_____

First finds feet

_____

Grips rattle or toy for the first time

_____

First looks in a mirror

First reaches out for you

First recognises name

First moves to music

First tooth

First haircut

First party invitation

First time on the potty

First dry day

First dry night

Lullaby

A peacefully sleeping baby is a vision of loveliness, a little angel. Some babies may seem more wakeful than others but in time parents hit on a winning bedtime formula. Sometimes it is a favourite story or song; or you may have to kiss umpteen toys goodnight! Eventually even the most determined baby will succumb, lulled by the stroking hand or the soothing voice of a loved one.

How long did your baby sleep each day:

at 1 week?_____   at 5 weeks?_____

at 2 weeks?_____   at 6 weeks?_____

at 3 weeks?_____   at 6 months?_____

at 4 weeks?_____   at 12 months?_____

When did baby first sleep through the night?

When did daytime naps stop?

First night in own room?

Did baby have a comforter?

Did baby have a favourite bedtime routine?

Favourite lullaby?

Describe baby's bedtime toys

Rub-a-dub-dub

There's much more to bathtime than simply washing. Ask any baby
about the happy, splashy time to be had in the tub. The simplest things can provide
endless fun — cups for pouring, bottles for squirting. As a special treat, add
a little bubble bath and let baby splash in the foam.

When did baby first enjoy a bath?　　　　　Use a big bath alone?
_____　　_____

Describe the first bath　　　　　What were baby's favourite bath toys?
_____　　_____

_____　　_____

When did baby first join you in the bath?　　And best loved bath time song?
_____　　_____

Photographs

Naming Day

The gathering of family and friends at baby's naming ceremony is a joyful tradition.

A christening evokes many joyous images. A baby in a flowing robe, ribbons on flowers, bows on gifts, church bells ringing out to welcome a newborn. Solemn vows are taken by parents and godparents, the people charged with helping to steer the child through life's passage. Family and friends love to gather for this spiritually significant occasion.
Some parents prefer a naming day, a less formal introduction to the world but equally heartfelt. For others, it's a party to honour the newcomer. Whichever you choose, it's a momentous day in a young life.

Baby's full name

Meaning of names

Date and place

Your baby wore

The celebration was held at

How did your baby react?

Guests

Presents

SPECIAL PEOPLE

✦ ✦ ✦

For baby, mum and dad are the centre of the world. The broadest grins and
most loving giggles are reserved for them. But others form an essential
circle of love, trust and friendship on which your baby will grow to depend.
There may be older brothers and sisters who will fascinate a young
baby with their antics. Also, there may be more siblings to come later.
Anyone your baby sees on a daily or weekly basis will soon forge a close
bond which will endure for the months and years ahead.
Remember those people your baby loved best here.

Brothers

Sisters

Aunts

Uncles

Neighbours

Nanny or carer

Other special friends

Photographs

Play Time

Children learn through play – and it's fun as well. In the early days mum and dad are the best gymnasium, providing support for shaky limbs. Soon household objects and toys will become a major source of interest, holding baby's rapt attention as balls roll, bricks stack, cupboards empty, water splashes. Then it's 'let's pretend', with baby suddenly a policeman or a ballerina, a doctor or nurse, a goody or baddy. It's hard to believe so much progress can be made in such a short time.

When did baby first play peek-a-boo?

First swipe at a hanging toy?

First go after a rolling ball?

First stack building bricks?

First look at a book?

First play a toy instrument?

First play a pretend game?

First use a swing?

First ride a tricycle?

Favourite Toys

✦ ✦ ✦

Who can tell which plaything will capture the imagination of your child? A garish purple dragon may seem the height of hideousness to you when to your child it is an object to be loved, petted and cuddled, no matter how chewed and dog-eared it becomes. It is not only fluffy animals that children seize on as favourites. Toy cars, wooden trains, rubber balls and even pint-sized vacuum cleaners may all become top of the popular toys, dragged up to bed and snuggled up to. Each will be christened and lavished with love.

Favourite fluffy toy

Its name

Favourite wheeled toy

Favourite toy at 3 months/9 months

Favourite toy at 18 months/2 years

Bedtime companion

Its name

Where did it come from?

Oddest 'toy'

Let's Go

◆ ◇ ◆

Stepping out of the door with baby for the first time is a proud moment —
even if it's taken hours to get ready. The simplest outing will provide
interest and stimulation for your baby, whether it is a walk in
the park, feeding the ducks or a trip to the local shop.
Record details of your first outing here.

Where did you go?

_____

How did baby travel?

_____

And what did your baby wear?

_____

Awake or asleep?

_____

First time in a buggy

_____

First time without a buggy

_____

First time on a bus

_____

First time on a train

_____

First time in the park

_____

First fed the ducks

_____

First visit to a playgroup

_____

First visit to a friend

_____

Other first outings/dates

First Foods

When milk alone is not enough to satisfy baby's hunger, it's time to start on solid food – an exciting, if messy, time.

First solid food served

_____

What was it?

_____

Where did baby sit?

_____

What was the reaction?

_____

Final breast or bottle feed

_____

Favourite meal at six months

_____

First finger food held at

_____

Spoon first held at

_____

First drank from a covered beaker	Favourite main meal
First drank from open cup	Favourite fruit
First meal in a cafe or restaurant	Most hated food
Favourite drink	Favourite treat

Happy Talk

✧ ✧ ✧

As soon as your baby arrives you launch into conversations but, of course, they are all one way! It doesn't take long, however, for your baby to discover the pleasures of creating sounds and he or she will soon want to chatter back, even if you cannot understand all that is being said.

As a parent you will learn to recognise the meaning of a full range of coos and grunts, even if no one else can. It is a wonderful moment when your baby begins to talk into a play telephone, one of their first departures into the land of make-believe.

When did baby first coo?

_____

When was the first repeated noise, like ga-ga?

_____

When was the first laugh?

And the first shout to attract your attention?

When did your baby start using a play telephone?

Record the date of the first word

And the first animal noise (moo, woof)

First Friends

✧ ✧

Playmates form an ever-increasing place of importance in your child's world. With another young one, they will learn the value of sharing toys, playing pretend and laughing too, at first alongside each other, then together. But when you are young anyone or anything can become a firm friend. A family cat or dog – or one that lives nearby – is often adored by a baby. There may be a toy or doll with whom he or she regularly chats. Some children even have an imaginary friend complete with name and appetite… you may find your child asking for two biscuits, one for himself and one for an invisible pal.

First boy friend

First girl friend

Best friend at 1 year

Best friend at 2 years

Cat

Dog

Other pets

Invisible friend

Photographs

Favourite Things

✦ ✧ ✦

It won't be long before your baby gives a clear indication of just what he or she likes – and loathes. Giving your baby the power of choice helps them to assert their budding characters. Attachments form quickly between a baby and toy, T-shirt, dinner dish or even a television programme. As for dislikes, they can range from food to hairwashing, teeth cleaning and even colours. Giving your child what he or she likes doesn't mean spoiling them. Children have preferences just as we do, and it is only natural to consider their views.

Favourite rough and tumble games

_____

Favourite soothing habit
eg thumb sucking

_____

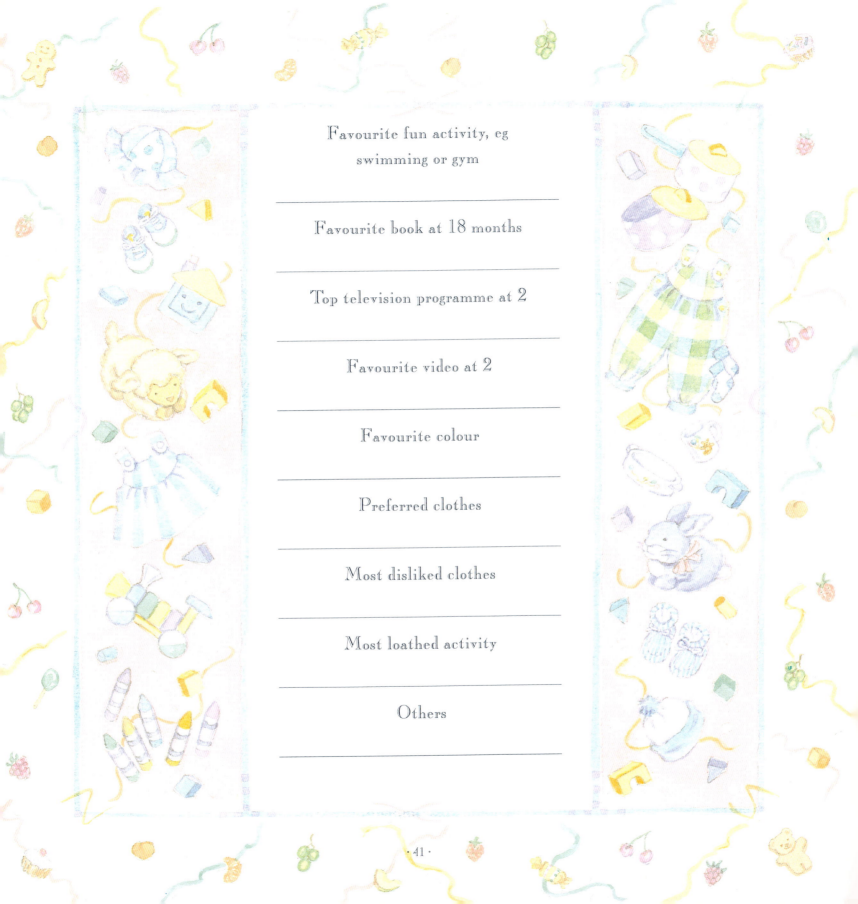

Favourite fun activity, eg swimming or gym

Favourite book at 18 months

Top television programme at 2

Favourite video at 2

Favourite colour

Preferred clothes

Most disliked clothes

Most loathed activity

Others

SUMMER FUN

Sea, frothy surf, soft sand and shells— the beach is a glorious adventure playground for your baby. Remember those first golden moments at the seaside here.

Date of first beach visit	First paddle
Where was it?	First sandcastle
Who came too?	First swim in the sea
Did baby like the water?	First collected shells
Did baby like the sand?	First donkey ride

SETTING OFF

✦ ◇ ✦

It's not much fun looking at the world from lying flat on your back. So it's not surprising that babies start a crusade to get on the move from when they are just a few weeks old. First step towards getting up and away happens at around two months, when they hold their heads up unsupported. From there it is on to rolling, sitting, crawling and then walking, which gives them a much-valued independence.

First holds head up

First roll

First press-up to tummy

Sits unsupported

Crawls

Stands holding onto something

Cruises around the furniture

Climbs the stairs

Walks unaided

ART WORK

From the moment babies grasp a crayon they are keen to make their mark. Paste your baby's first drawing on the next page. Don't forget to date it!

When did your baby first hold a crayon?

_____

Make a scribble?

_____

Use finger paints?

_____

Use play dough?

_____

Use a paint brush?

_____

Hold a pencil 'properly'?

_____

Do a recognisable drawing?

_____

Draw a face?

_____

Draw a body?

_____

Sign his own drawing?

_____

First work of art

Party Pieces

All the world's a stage to a growing baby, who will thrive on showing off the latest tricks to an appreciative audience.

First waves bye-bye
_____

First claps hands
_____

First jumps
_____

Recites first nursery rhyme
_____

Sings first song
_____

Removes bits of clothing, eg socks
_____

Puts on clothing unaided
_____

Dresses up
_____

First dances	Others
First practical joke	
First pretends	

· Photographs ·

CELEBRATIONS

Introducing your baby to the traditions you love is a vital ritual and one you will enjoy. Suddenly, you see age-old celebrations through new eyes, as your baby does. Babies bring a delightful extra dimension to a festivity that everyone can share. Monitor their every response, from the elation of tasting a first chocolate Easter egg to the wonder of gazing through a window as fireworks burst in the sky above. For them it is only the beginning of a childhood in which they will look forward to every year's special dates with relish.

What happened on Mothers Day?   What happened on Father's Day?

_____   _____

And Mother's birthday?   And Father's birthday?

_____   _____

How did you celebrate baby's first Easter?

Where, and who was there?

How did you mark Firework night?

Other important festivals during baby's first year

Photographs

The First Noel

Christmas is for children and even the smallest baby will make the festive celebrations complete. The enchantment on their faces when they see a Christmas tree for the first time spangled with twinkling lights, glittering tinsel and shiny baubles is enough to make any heart lurch.

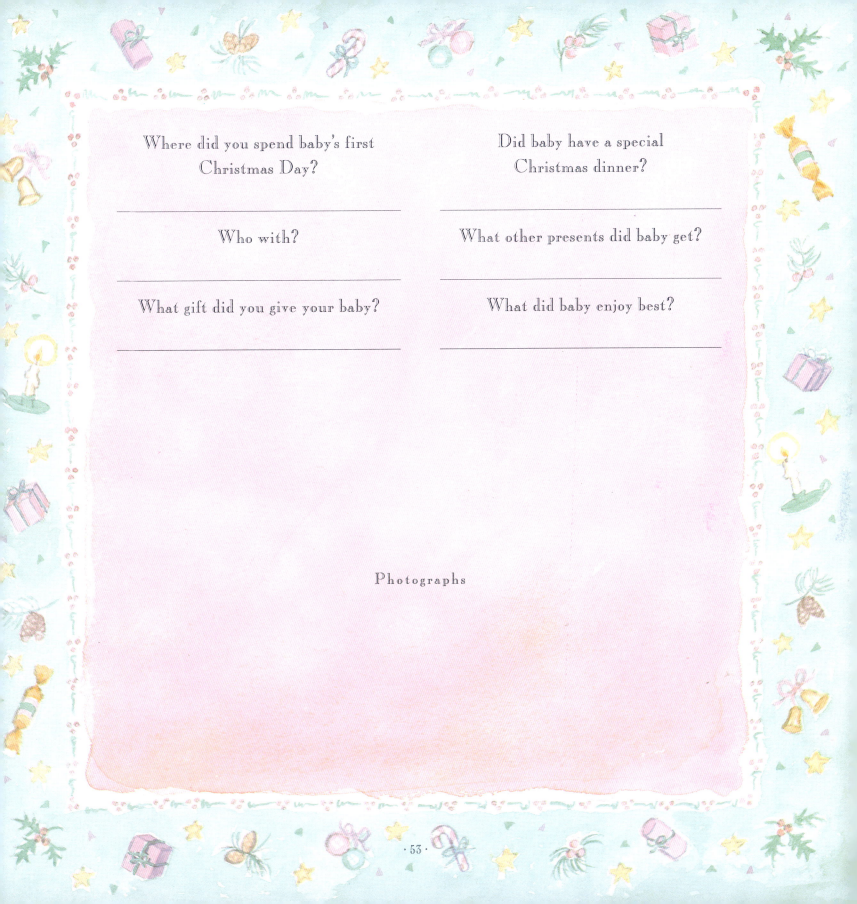

Where did you spend baby's first Christmas Day?

Who with?

What gift did you give your baby?

Did baby have a special Christmas dinner?

What other presents did baby get?

What did baby enjoy best?

Photographs

Happy Birthday to You

✧ ◇ ✧

It's astonishing how soon this special day arrives. For most mums, it seems like only weeks ago that the newborn was lying tiny and helpless in a cot. Twelve months on and they are robust, rampaging tots with plenty of skills already mastered, just waiting for the next challenge. They may not know what all the fuss is about but their little eyes will still shine at the sight of a cake, a candle and a chorus of 'Happy Birthday'. Spend a few quiet moments alone as well, to reflect on the first year of your baby's life.

How did you celebrate?

_____

Where?

_____

Who was there?

_____

_____

_____

What did you buy baby?

_____

What other gifts arrived?

_____

What was your baby's reaction?

_____

Describe the cake

_____

How did you feel?

_____

Photographs

PREDICTIONS

From the moment you become pregnant, you are full of hopes and dreams for your baby. If your pregnant bump was a lively little mover you will probably already have picked a future for it on the football field or disco dancing floor. In the early days it is a parent's prerogative to toy with careers and vocations for the newborn. There may even be family traditions which you hope they will follow. Write down what you want for them and why and capture those dreams forever. Then when your child makes its own way in the world you can compare your first thoughts with what has actually happened. In a few years ask your child what he or she imagines the future holds. The thoughts of a child, often quaint and curious, will make emotive reading, especially when they have children of their own.

Your Predictions

Your Child's Predictions

Medical Records

✧ ✧ ✧

For the health and well-being of your baby, keep a note of the illnesses contracted and the immunisations received. Remember, immunisation timetables may vary around the country.

✧ VACCINATIONS ✧

Triple vaccine (diphtheria, tetanus and whooping cough)

First injection _____

Second injection _____

Third injection _____

Measles, mumps and rubella

_____

Polio

_____

Hib

_____

BCG

Booster for diphtheria, tetanus, whooping cough and polio (pre-school)

❖ ILLNESSES ❖

Chicken pox

Measles or mumps

Allergies (and reactions)

NHS number

Other notes

GROWING UP

Record your baby's height and weight with two different coloured lines
on the chart opposite. Sometimes your baby will shoot up from one month
to the next – at other times you will worry that there is no progress!
But by the end of the first year you will be astonished by the
progress of your infant.

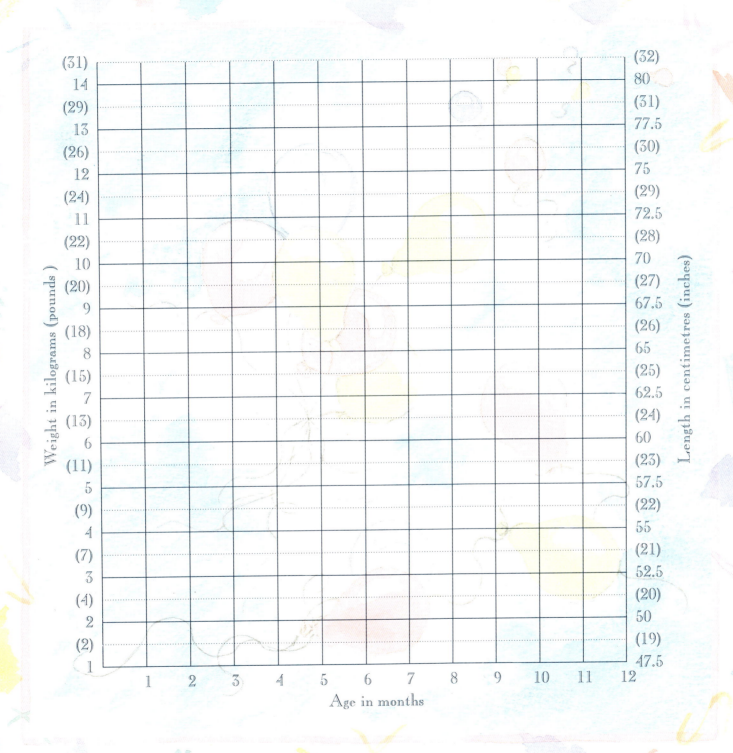

Copyright © Bookmart Ltd 1993

First published as a book & tape set 1997

This book created by Amazon Publishing Ltd
Design by Meryl Lloyd
Typeset by The R&B Partnership

All rights reserved. No part of this publication may be reproduced, stored in a retrieval system, or transmitted in any form, or by any means electronic, mechanical, photocopying, recording or otherwise without prior written permission from the publishers.

Published by Abbeydale Press, an imprint of Bookmart Ltd, Registered Number 2372865. Trading as Bookmart Limited, Desford Road, Enderby, Leicester LE9 5AD

ISBN 1-86147-008-8

Printed in Singapore